BELOVED CHILD

MARIAM NALUBOWA.

Copyright © 2020 by Mariam Nalubowa.

All rights reserved. No part of this publication may be reproduced, distributed or transmitted in any form or by any means, including photocopying, recording, or other electronic or mechanical methods, without the prior written permission of the publisher, except in the case of brief quotations embodied in critical reviews and certain other noncommercial uses permitted by copyright law.

Paperback : 978-1-7355344-2-8

Hardback : 978-1-7355344-3-5

Epub: 978-1-7355344-4-2

VOCABULARY

Commotion - Violent noisy disturbance

Racism - Discrimination based on race

Pandemic - Outbreak of a diseases over the whole world

Complexion - The natural color and appearance of a person's skin

Nesh was 10 years old. Sundays used to be her favorite day of the week because she got to visit grandpa. She would get dropped off at her grandparent's house every Sunday morning but recently things had changed.

There was no more going to school, parks and visiting because of a pandemic. She liked being home schooled but dearly missed seeing her friends and grandparents.

She had also noticed there was a lot of discussions and commotion about racism and was confused.

SHE HAD ALSO NOTICED THERE WAS A LOT OF DISCUSSIONS AND COMMOTION ABOUT BLACK LIVES AND WAS CONFUSED.

BLM?

SHE NEVER THOUGHT OF HERSELF AS BLACK OR WHITE OR ANYTHING OTHER THAN BEING HER FATHER AND MOTHER'S DAUGHTER.

She never thought of herself as black or white or anything other than being her father and mother's daughter.

She was her grandparents' grandchild.

She was her brother's big sister.
She was also Mark`s best friend.

She liked to wear her hair in braids. She was pretty with a brown skin complexion and she knew she was loved by her family and friends.

Grandpa always calls at 2pm. Nesh thought, I must ask him about it. The phone rang and when she picked up, she asked "Grandpa am I black?"

Grandpa knew that Nesh loved ladybird beetles and so to answer her question, he told her a story using ladybird beetles as the main characters gathering for a party.

He said "Nesh, one day pink spotted ladybird organized a house warming party and invited all neighboring beetles to her house. She had mites, insect eggs and cups full of pollen for snacks. She puts up a big sign that read COLEOMEGILLA MACULATA`S House Warming Party."

The roller rolled in. He doesn't look like me, pink spotted ladybird thought to herself and then asked "Are you a black ladybird beetle?". He replied "No, my name is Scarab, I am a dung beetle from Kenya. I roll dung for long distances with my hind legs. I use it as a food source and a place for my wife to lay her eggs. My body is dark and round with six strong legs." With a warm smile pink spotted ladybug beetle replied "You are welcome to my house Scarab. You are such a strong beetle to roll dung that's so much bigger than you are."

Pink spotted ladybird heard a lot of beetle voices talking at the door. She welcomed them in but was surprised at what she saw.

"You have large orange bodies", she said to a group of Asian ladybird beetles. Yes, they replied "We like to gather in large groups and sit on warm reflective surfaces like windows. We also bite and leave foul smelling liquid on surfaces where we gather. We are sometimes brown. Some of us have black spots on our wings, just like you, and others don't have any spots, but we all have a big M-shaped black mark on our white heads. We are called Harmonia axyridis."

Pink spotted ladybird beetle
sat them at the shiny window
and they were so happy.

Two yellow ladybird beetles walked in. Pink spotted ladybird said to them "Hello, you look like cucumbers and I like your cucumber body shape." One of the yellow cucumber ladybirds replied, "I have 12 black spots and I am called Diabrotica Howardi, my brother has an oval body with three black strips on a yellow abdomen with short legs. He is called Acalymma vittatum and we love to eat cucumbers."

Chilocorus stigma walked in, she looked elegant. Pink spotted ladybird was amazed. "Hi Stigma" she said with a big smile. "You look a bit like Roller the dung beetle but you are different because you have a different shade of black. Your coat is so shinny and you have two red spots on each wing. You are beautiful." "Thank you for noticing", said Stigma the black shiny ladybird.

Goldenrod solider beetle arrived at the party. He carried his long soft body around gently. He was hungry. He wanted to eat some maggots, small caterpillars and vegetables because that's his favorite food. Pink spotted ladybird beetle ordered for some yummy small caterpillars for her neighbor.

Some white ladybird beetles walked in. One looked pale, she was an albino, pink spotted ladybug noticed. Another one was white with 15 black spots, one had 20 spots and another was ashy grey. She gave them all a warm welcoming hug.

That evening Pink spotted ladybird looked around and noticed that her neighbors were of different shades of color, body sizes and shapes and they all liked to eat different foods, but regardless of the differences they were all ladybird beetles. She loved them and was happy to have them as neighbors. She then looked at herself and noticed that her body was of medium size oblong. It was pink marked with black spots. She was happy with herself.

"Nesh, you are our beloved child and the world to us." her grandpa said.

Grandpa continued "Just like your favorite ladybirds, every one of us is different yet the same. We are all wonderful in our own ways."

Nesh felt so much better because she understood that she was as wonderful as everybody else and knew that her complexion, body size and shape did not matter. She was her parents Beloved child and the world.

THE END

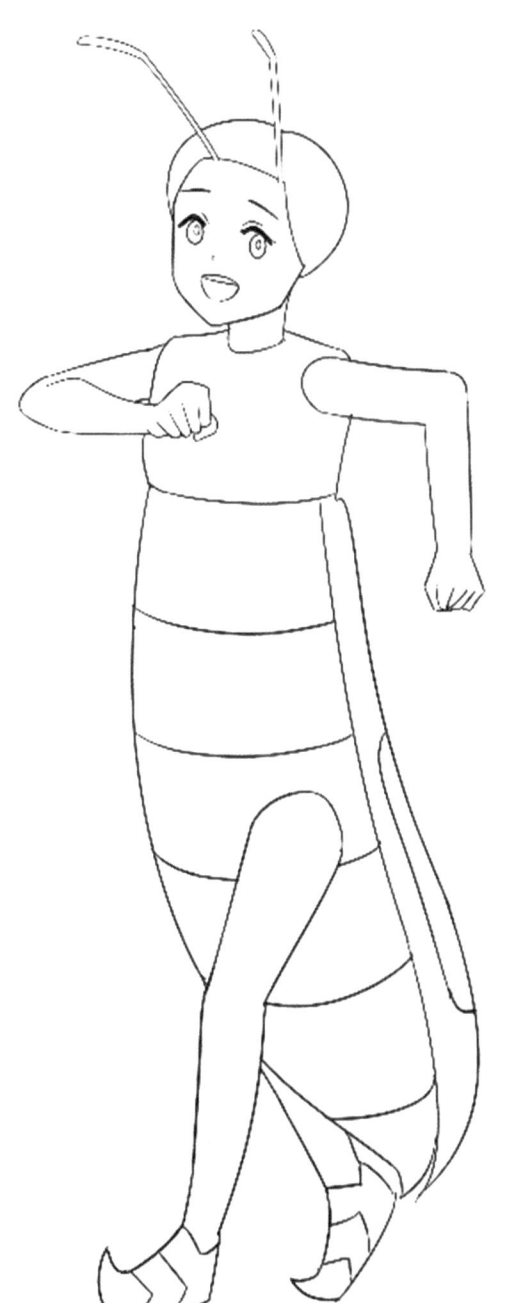

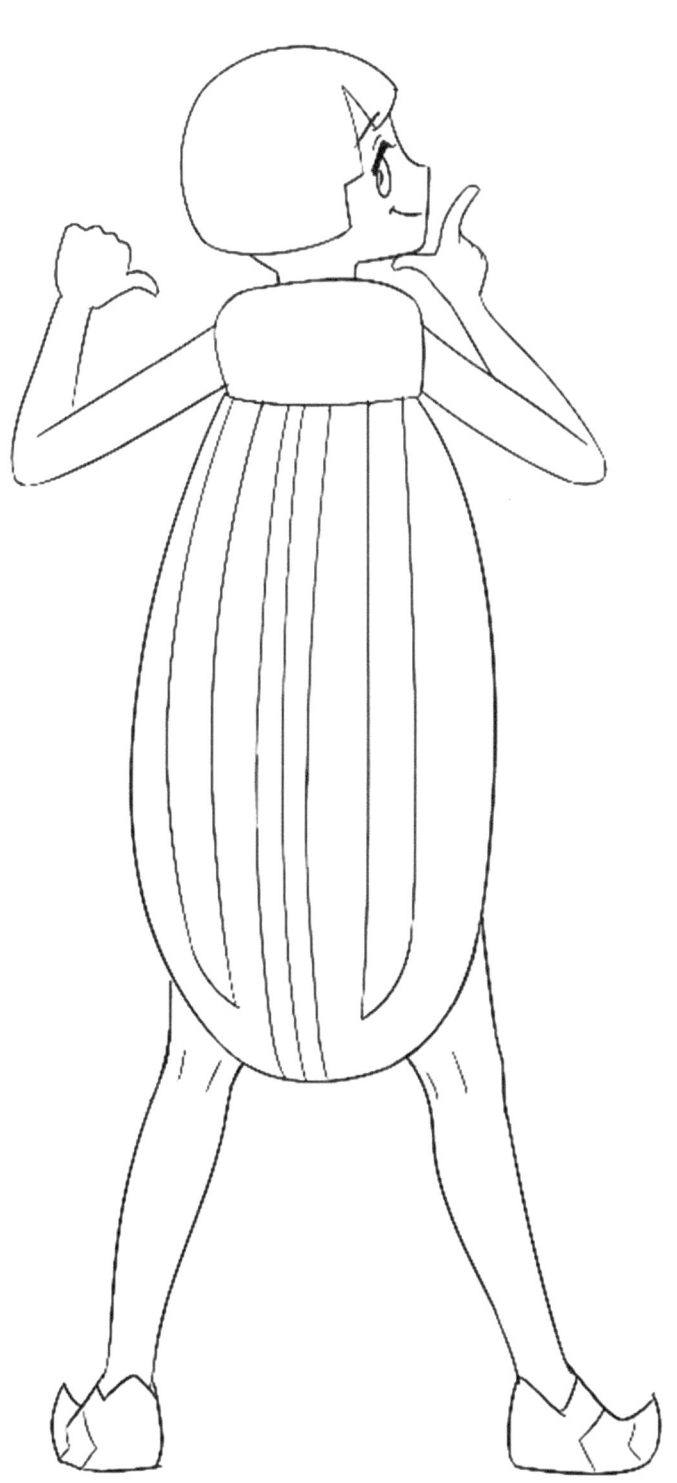

www.ingramcontent.com/pod-product-compliance
Lightning Source LLC
Chambersburg PA
CBHW040002110526
44587CB00001BA/29